WALKING IS A WAY OF KNOWING

In a Kadar Forest

Madhuri Ramesh

Manish Chandi

Matthew Frame

TARA BOOKS

ENTERING THE FOREST

It is always dark inside the forest and the sky is green. The sunlight filters through the layers of leaves and lights them up in parakeet green, fern green, viper green, and dark spinach green. Only here and there does it reach all the way down, past the leaves, to glint off a rock.

Forest trails are uneven, winding routes, and I took time to get used to them. At first I walked like a child, stumbling every few feet though my eyes were on the ground. But after a few weeks, with constant practice, I moved swiftly, without having to think about the next step.

There are pillars of trees with thick curving roots that wind across the path just to trip up newcomers like me. The paths are narrow and muddy; they swerve round huge trunks, go a little down-slope and then slant upwards again – very 'snaky' sort of paths. The older ones are well-worn, scuffed bare by feet and there are no grasses or herbs growing on them. They are wide enough to walk on without dew-laden leaves brushing my shoulders.

There are no large spider webs either, to softly and spookily stick to my face or glint like silver in the greenish light. The newer paths and the less used ones are narrower since there is just enough space to place one foot carefully in front of the other. These are tiring paths, especially if it is a steep climb, because I can't even stand comfortably at any point. Usually my chest heaves and I struggle to breathe before I go very far, but Madiyappan, my elderly companion, keeps walking and says calmly,

"This is how all paths are first made."

While I stop to drink water, he goes on,

"Paths have character: there are easy ones, challenging ones, unforgiving ones, ones that encourage you to walk with a steady swinging rhythm and others that tease your stride with odd twists and turns."

He points in the direction of the broad trail we left behind earlier and says,

"Paths also speak of the kinds of people who walk on them: the Kadar paths are confident, well-worn and wide. The Malai Malasars' are shy; rarely more than narrow, grassy trails like those made by jungle fowl – their paths often go across marshes and swift streams, making it hard for anyone else to pursue them. You have to be sure-footed to walk fast on such paths."

He shakes his head in disapproval as he begins to walk again.

"The mahouts, those Malasars from the plains, they create large paths more than two feet across, almost like the broad tar roads in Valparai! They and their elephants strip the trees bare as they go to and fro, so you'll rarely see an animal or bird along those routes."

I ask Madiyappan if he ever feels lonely or scared in the forest, because unlike the others who go in twos and threes, he often walks alone with just a machete in hand.

He says "They chatter all the time! But I, I like to pause for a minute after entering the forest." He watches a whistling thrush on a branch ahead as he continues softly: "I like to see if anyone has walked on that path recently, to check if my ancestors are walking with me in the form of these *muthiyarthiyar* that call "phee... phee...". Sometimes they are with me as I enter, and sometimes they'll meet me further along the way. So I'm never alone."

FINDING ONE'S WAY

Since Madiyappan often goes into the forest by himself and returns safely, all the Kadars agree that he has an excellent sense of direction. So on another day, when we both went with his cousin Padma (the one who can speak five languages!) to fetch water from a stream, I asked him how he finds his way around. He said,

"I walk in the forest at all times of the day and in all seasons. The stars are of no use under this green sky, and even the trees and hills change appearance if it is misty or raining. Summer's forest fires can make a favourite path seem like a trek through a totally strange land. In the monsoon, even a well-worn trail can get hidden by a fallen tree or fresh grass and look unfamiliar – one can lose one's way in no time at all." He paused to scratch his leg with the tip of his machete.

"Knowing the path alone is not enough; how it cuts across the hills is important because sometimes, there will be elephants or gaur right on the path where it leads into a valley with a stream.

Then a person should know how to go off into the forest above the valley and return to the path further on. Or which paths will be infested with leeches after heavy rains. Or which ones meander among the teak trees and leave you hot and itching with tick bites in summer."

We reached the river, and Padma began scrubbing the pots with sand to clean them before filling them with water.

Even Madiyappan's speech reminds me of the forest trails he spends so much time on, for it meanders gently and touches upon many interesting things before taking me to the answer. So I asked him again,

"But how do you not get lost? Even while coming and going on the same path, I sometimes get confused because things look different in this hilly place."

I pointed out a large *kungilium* tree nearby that was visible when we walked down-hill but would be hidden by other leaves when we climbed uphill. Then Padma explained,

"People who are good at finding their way in the forest always scan the area every now and then. It becomes a habit with them, like the way animals sniff around every few feet. And their feet record the feel of the path: a stone or an exposed root in the way, a tangle of lianas that they stepped over, the slippery

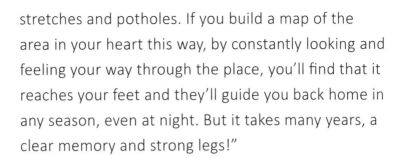

stretches and potholes. If you build a map of the area in your heart this way, by constantly looking and feeling your way through the place, you'll find that it reaches your feet and they'll guide you back home in any season, even at night. But it takes many years, a clear memory and strong legs!"

As we helped Padma fill the pots, Madiyappan added that people who walk in the forest often leave small signs that can help them find their way back – they break a branch at an angle, or lop a shrub with a clean stroke.

"I don't idly hack at trees with my machete: I make small notches that will tell my hands even at dusk whether I am on the right trail or not. How do I know which signs are mine and not just the roughness of the bark? My cuts have clean, smooth edges whereas natural cuts are jagged. That's how I find my way in the forest – by using everything I have – eyes, legs and hands." He continued to talk as we returned to the settlement.

"Whenever we gather together and chat, whether outside our huts or at the bus stop, we often learn new routes or remember ones we haven't used in a while. We learn simply by listening to who went where that day. To you, it will sound very strange when I tell my brother, 'Today when looking for honey, I turned left off the teak tree path and walked along the stream where

Padma and my wife wash clothes every day. That route took me along the bamboo patch to the valley with nettles. Then I climbed up, onto the path to Kadavusathy and came back the other way.'

"In a forest full of trees, how do you know which teak tree I am talking about? Which of the hundred forest streams do Padma and my wife wash their clothes in? Only a Kadar can really understand another Kadar's route because we have some regular routes, or some trees or rocks or locations that we all know clearly; places with a story around them."

Though they often argue, this time Padma agreed with him as we stacked the pots inside her house.

"Every time we sit together and share stories, old and new, we're adding to each other's map of the forest. For instance, if he made a new path near the old teak tree, at least one of us would go off and investigate this new shortcut we'd heard about, wouldn't we? If it is a good one, many of us will gradually begin to use it. If it isn't, there will be much argument and discussion the next time we all gather around to talk. "Good forest people are curious, we constantly explore. We often do it for fun, but it can save our lives if we ever lose our way or it is blocked by an elephant or a bear. At such times you cannot take the straightest route home, and this knowledge makes all the difference."

INSIDE
THE FOREST

Last month, I almost saw a leopard at the bus stop. I say 'almost' because it was early in the morning and the mist had not lifted yet when I heard a leopard cough somewhere behind me. I couldn't see it but I definitely heard it.

Madiyappan came to the bus stop a little later and when I told him about the leopard, he said, "Ears can hear further into a forest than eyes can see because not just the spirits but even the birds and monkeys can hide their forms from you, but never the sound of their breathing. So it's important to keep your ears open at all times. In fact, that's why *Kadavul* gave lids for our eyes but none for our ears!"

That reminded me of a conversation I had with Madiyappan's uncle, Krishnan, in Valparai last year. Many of our conversations begin as arguments because Krishnan has worked with many researchers and feels he knows everything about everything!

Anyway, we were arguing about a bird call we heard and, when he realised I'd been right all along, he changed the subject. "Everyone knows the sound of

the birds, barking deer, leopard, elephant and gaur but only the attentive hear the trees."

He beat the handle of his machete against a tall buttressed tree and said that people passed on messages in this manner in the old days. He said the sound of an axe cutting into the wood is different because it is not so resonant — it ends with a dull 'thuk' sound. (I must remember to check with Madiyappan if this is true.)

Then we counted off on our fingers all the other tree sounds we could think of: Dead trees topple with a loud, prolonged crash and their roots make a great tearing sound.

When monkeys bounce on a branch in play, it breaks with a sharp dry snap; this is different from the tearing papery sound that tree barks and green branches make when elephants strip them away to eat.

The trees whisper when the langurs move silently and rapidly from one tree to the other: a soft, swishy sound like a breeze blowing towards you. But Krishnan laughed at me when I said it sounds exactly like the sea from a distance. He can be an irritating person. However, he told me an interesting story about a humming tree.

"Once, when I was young, I heard a tree hum. I put my head close to the trunk I was resting against and heard a deep thrumming sound.

I thought there was some spirit hiding in the tree so I walked around and squinted at it closely, my machete ready in my hand. I saw a small dark opening above my head and when I poked it with a stick, some bees flew out and stung me: the hollow contained *kurun thelli*, a small beehive. That was the humming sound! I was so relieved that it wasn't a spirit of some sort because spirits are troublesome things and it is better to not disturb them, even by accident. I didn't take any honey from those bees, though I could have used it later to cure my children's coughs and colds in the rainy season."

The Kadars identify four types of hives: *perun thaen* or *thaen thelli* found on cliffs and large trees, *ponthu thaen* or kurun thelli in the hollows of tree trunks, *kombu thaen* or *kohtaan*, which are found in small hollows at the base of trees, and *kosuru thaen* or *karun thelli* made by very tiny bees in rock hollows. Each has different medicinal properties. I would like to sketch the hives some time.

Actually, you can not only hear the trees but you can also read them. I've noticed fist-sized knobs going up the trees, from about the height of my head right to the top. They are common on the emergents (the tall trees that

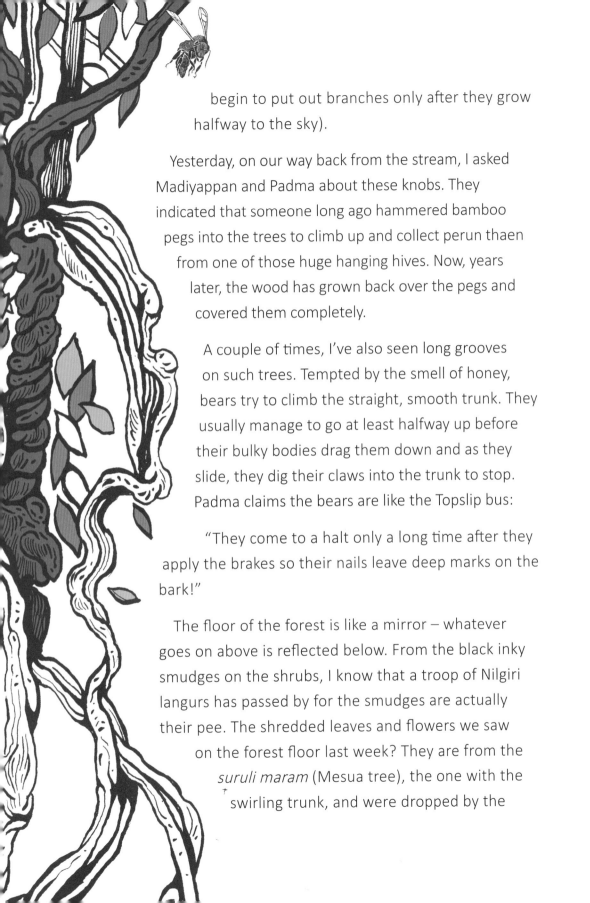

begin to put out branches only after they grow halfway to the sky).

Yesterday, on our way back from the stream, I asked Madiyappan and Padma about these knobs. They indicated that someone long ago hammered bamboo pegs into the trees to climb up and collect perun thaen from one of those huge hanging hives. Now, years later, the wood has grown back over the pegs and covered them completely.

A couple of times, I've also seen long grooves on such trees. Tempted by the smell of honey, bears try to climb the straight, smooth trunk. They usually manage to go at least halfway up before their bulky bodies drag them down and as they slide, they dig their claws into the trunk to stop. Padma claims the bears are like the Topslip bus:

"They come to a halt only a long time after they apply the brakes so their nails leave deep marks on the bark!"

The floor of the forest is like a mirror – whatever goes on above is reflected below. From the black inky smudges on the shrubs, I know that a troop of Nilgiri langurs has passed by for the smudges are actually their pee. The shredded leaves and flowers we saw on the forest floor last week? They are from the *suruli maram* (Mesua tree), the one with the swirling trunk, and were dropped by the

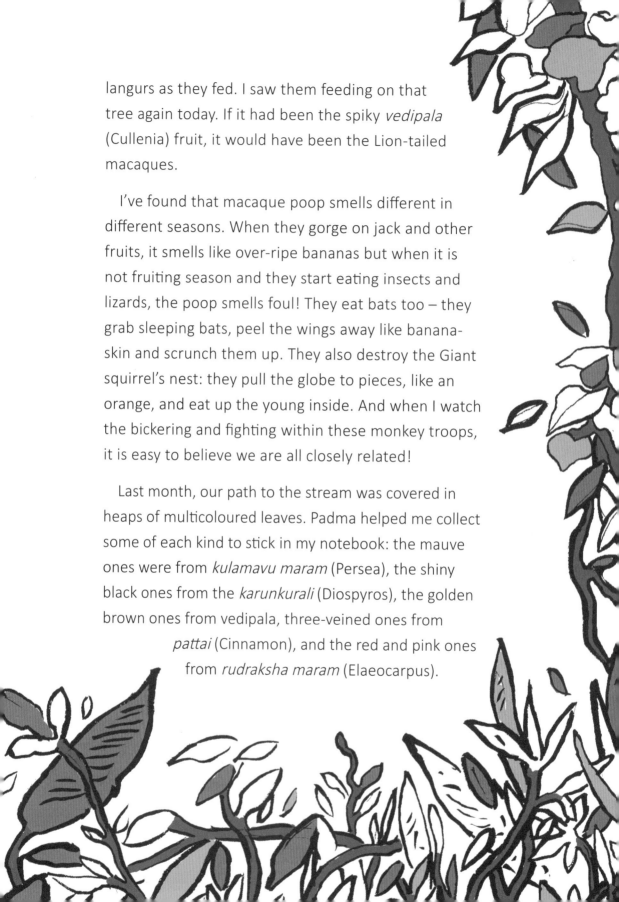

langurs as they fed. I saw them feeding on that tree again today. If it had been the spiky *vedipala* (Cullenia) fruit, it would have been the Lion-tailed macaques.

I've found that macaque poop smells different in different seasons. When they gorge on jack and other fruits, it smells like over-ripe bananas but when it is not fruiting season and they start eating insects and lizards, the poop smells foul! They eat bats too – they grab sleeping bats, peel the wings away like banana-skin and scrunch them up. They also destroy the Giant squirrel's nest: they pull the globe to pieces, like an orange, and eat up the young inside. And when I watch the bickering and fighting within these monkey troops, it is easy to believe we are all closely related!

Last month, our path to the stream was covered in heaps of multicoloured leaves. Padma helped me collect some of each kind to stick in my notebook: the mauve ones were from *kulamavu maram* (Persea), the shiny black ones from the *karunkurali* (Diospyros), the golden brown ones from vedipala, three-veined ones from *pattai* (Cinnamon), and the red and pink ones from *rudraksha maram* (Elaeocarpus).

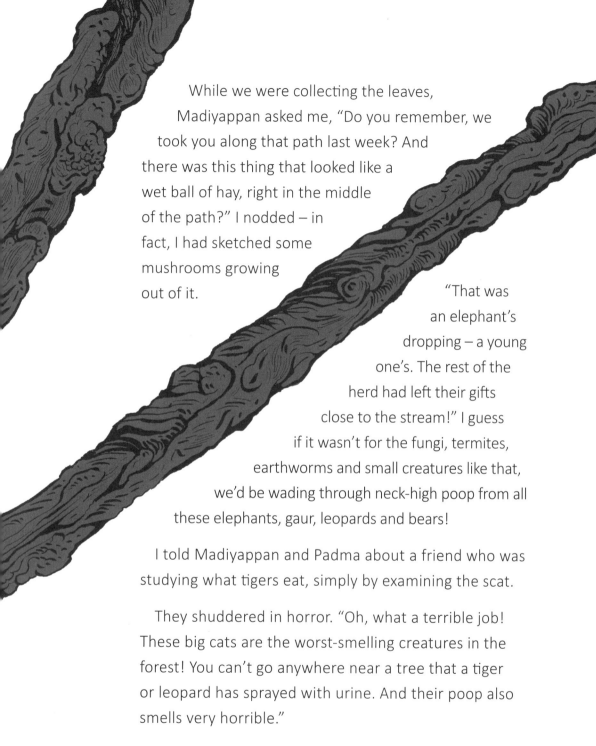

While we were collecting the leaves, Madiyappan asked me, "Do you remember, we took you along that path last week? And there was this thing that looked like a wet ball of hay, right in the middle of the path?" I nodded – in fact, I had sketched some mushrooms growing out of it.

"That was an elephant's dropping – a young one's. The rest of the herd had left their gifts close to the stream!" I guess if it wasn't for the fungi, termites, earthworms and small creatures like that, we'd be wading through neck-high poop from all these elephants, gaur, leopards and bears!

I told Madiyappan and Padma about a friend who was studying what tigers eat, simply by examining the scat.

They shuddered in horror. "Oh, what a terrible job! These big cats are the worst-smelling creatures in the forest! You can't go anywhere near a tree that a tiger or leopard has sprayed with urine. And their poop also smells very horrible."

And then Padma whispered to me, "People's poop stinks too! Ours smell as bad as the cats' so I like to cover mine up with a bit of mud and leaf litter." I've noticed that bear poop, though it looks like human poop, doesn't smell as bad. Maybe it's because they mostly eat tubers and fruits.

When we were drinking strong black tea outside his house, I showed Madiyappan my sketch of the mushrooms.

He had a story for that too.

"My neighbours found a patch of white kumin last year, close to the *naaval* maram right behind our village. But they weren't the first. A jungle fowl had already scratched around at one end and fed on some. And next to that, there were some nibbled remains, which were a sign that a tortoise had walked that way earlier that morning."

When I commented that jungle fowl were noisy birds, he teased me.

"Outsiders like you walk like jungle fowl when they enter the forest: they move in spurts and are noisy, the leaf litter goes all *surra burra surra burra*, whereas we walk silently and firmly like the elephants. Yes, that is a strange thing about elephants. Despite their size they move without a sound when they want to and their bodies just merge into the forest. So, very often, to spot elephants you actually have to look down at the ground for telltale signs or sniff the air from all four directions — they have a distinctive smell."

So what Padma told me that day is true – Madiyappan does stand in the middle of the forest and sniff all around to see what's coming! When he saw me hurriedly scribbling down what he said, Madiyappan got impatient.

"The forest is like a storehouse of smells; how can you learn about the scent of the civet, leopard, tiger or gaur from talk? These are things that you can know only directly. People like you, from other places, use books to understand the forest, so you know things from the pictures and the words and recognise them only by sight.

"Most of us can't read a word, but we use all our senses, our entire body, to hear the stories of the forest. We can smell the smoke of a forest fire and feel gusts of its fierce heat much before we see it. In fact, if we can see it, it probably means that we are much too close to it! But don't worry, you're beginning to acquire the forest ways. You shuffle just like a bear when you're tired!"

Ah, so first I was a jungle fowl and now, a bear. And when I get impatient, he tells me my eyes and nose turn red like a Cane turtle!

Then Padma's sister Shanti came by and asked me to guess what the faint spicy smell on her hands was. I was puzzled until Madiyappan reminded me,

"The small valley we crossed yesterday when we went to look for the hornbills? There are wild ginger and turmeric plants there. When you spend a few hours digging them up, you can smell them on your hands even as you sleep at night."

I can recognise many other smells too. When piles of leaf litter get wet in the rain and slowly dry out over a few days, they give off a decomposing sort of smell. Then there's the muddy smell of mushroom, the loud ripeness of jack fruit and bread fruit. And a glossy, dark green shrub whose leaves smell like green chillies.

Krishnan joined our conversation about smells and said, "I would like to turn into a pattai maram when I die. It is fragrant even when it is dead and rotting with termites and molds busily turning it to powder." But Shanti disagreed.

"The *sambarani* smells even better. Can you see the large one on the crest of the hill opposite us, with the pink, orange and red leaves? If you cut the bark with your machete on your way into the forest, the dark reddish brown resin will slowly ooze out and dry up into chunks that you can collect on your way back."

Madiyappan showed me a piece he had in his house, and it gleamed like a jewel when I held it up to the sun. "You should go home and light this with a small piece of coal, the smoke smells wonderful! This and turmeric, honey and ginger, are all part of the wealth that Kadavul gave the Kadars."

HOME IN THE FOREST

I ate lunch in Padma's house yesterday because she had cooked raw jack fruit curry specially for me. Of course, Shanti and Madiyappan were also there. So was Krishnan, who had come from Valparai two days earlier to attend a funeral feast in Erumaparai. They all told me about how the gaur had come right inside the settlement the previous night and stood there, stamping and snorting for hours. But no one seemed very worried or frightened. In fact, Shanti only complained that the gaur had crushed her hibiscus plant and now it would take weeks for it to flower again. I asked her,

"Aren't you ever frightened of the animals or the forest? Even at night?"

She shrugged and said, "We grew up here in Karian Shola, the dark forest. Our fathers, grandfathers, all roamed this area, and we know every stream and hill like you know every room in your house. We think of the forest as home; a place where we have everything we need and a place that makes us feel good."

Madiyappan dramatically held up the small white cloth bag he carries everywhere and told me, "I need very little to survive inside this Karian Shola. Do you carry bundles and bundles of things when you go home? Or when you go away from home?"

One by one, he took out the things in his bag and laid them on the floor next to me. "Here's a box of matches to light a fire, some soapnuts to make a paste to keep the leeches away and my machete, which is like my right hand. Sometimes I carry a torch."

And then he put them all away in his bag again.
"Amongst our people, an expert in junglecraft is one who understands the forest well and can live off it. But for others, it seems a tough place to live in, a place to be feared."

Padma waved her hand towards the jackfruit trees behind her house.

"There's food here and drinking water, places to sit, climb, swim and sleep. There are even plates and tumblers and clothing if you know where to look!"

I've seen the Kadar people stitch together the brown papery spathes of the bamboo plant to be used as plates. Or the leaves of teak or wild banana plants.

She said, "Earlier, we used lengths of bamboo stems as water bottles. There's also another tree I've heard the elders talk about – I've forgotten its name now but it has reddish bark that you can pull off like a sheet and wrap around you!"

We had discussed this idea of home earlier too, when we had trekked to Valparai. That day, Madiyappan pointed out a makeshift hut near the trail and said the owner had gotten tired of living there and had gone back to living in the forest.

I insisted, "Everyone needs a home."

But Madiyappan disagreed with me. "Why do you need walls or a roof? Today that patch of forest there can be my bedroom and tomorrow, it could be my bathroom. Why, it can even be my bedroom and your kitchen simultaneously – you can light your cooking fire right here, between these small stones while I take a nap on the sheet rock there. Of course, there are difficulties too: if one falls ill, for instance. But the forest both creates problems and holds the solutions. For every fever you get in the forest, there is also a herb that can cure it." He waved his machete around and said, "You just have to know where to look – the answers are all there."

"But what about Erumaparai? Then why do you live in that settlement?"

"True, as you remind me, my *cheri* is Erumaparai, where I have a hut with mud walls and a bamboo-thatched roof. But my home is not complete without the forest surrounding it. Look, it is something like the way the *ongal* have gathered on this fig tree. These Great hornbills have come here from different places to eat the fruit, and maybe to gossip and tell each other what else is fruiting, in which valley. We too do that in the evenings when we cluster around the jack fruit trees in our cheri.

"Someone may have gone to Valparai and will bring news about our relatives there; someone may have gone to the tea *kadai* in Topslip and will talk about who they met there; someone else may have gone to Pollachi and will complain of how hot it is in the plains; someone may have found a perun thaen and will announce their claim... if the forest was a large house, I guess the cheri is like a verandah where people can sit around and talk."

But yesterday he said,

"We've lived here for so many generations that all the animals in this area know our smell and will mostly go their own way and not bother us. One must always be alert, of course, but the animals can tell who is from here and who is an outsider. I think this is because we bathe in the forest streams, scrubbing ourselves with fine sand instead of soap, and we eat a lot of tubers and drink stream water. Our bodies probably smell like the forest itself and that's why the animals don't get disturbed by our presence."

Then Krishnan, who had been listening to our conversation, said,

"Earlier, the Kadar people used to live in different patches of the forest for weeks at a time – to dig up tubers, collect honey, or find turmeric and other medicinal plants to sell to or barter with the plainspeople. We used

to trade with the world beyond the hills even before the British people came to cut down the big trees and sell them in the plains. Our people used to enter the forest swinging their machetes and carrying only a few things with them, like the flintstone, a blanket, or an empty tin or bamboo bottle. But when they came out, they would be laden with forest products.

"When I was younger, I too used to go in for days at a time. If I was going honey-hunting, I would go with my wife, my wife's brother or even by myself since I don't have any siblings. I'd make bamboo pegs one day, from the fresh green bamboo near the streams and hammer them all the way up the tall straight tree with the honeycomb. Then I would wait till nightfall the next day to climb up and cut down the part of the hive that contains honey.

"Only fools cut down the entire hive: what is the point? If you leave the part where the bees live intact, they will rebuild the store rooms of their hive soon and you can get honey from the same hive the next season too. But if you cut down the entire hive, all the bees die and you have to search for honey all over the forest! Before climbing up the tree at night, I would strap a clean kerosene tin to my back using ropes cut from canes or climbers and make a torch by binding rags around some green bamboo and dousing it with kerosene before setting it alight. At the bee-laden branch, I would first cover my face with my towel while smoking the bees out by burning a bunch of green leaves I had carried in my pocket. By this time, the torch would have burnt itself out. Then sitting on the branch, I would gently and carefully, cut down the hive. It is easier when there's moonlight. Honey sits heavy in the tin and in the stomach, so climbing down from that great height with a heavy load strapped to your back is a real challenge."

Madiyappan nodded in agreement.

"If you take even a peep at the ground below, your head will spin and you could fall down and die. Honey-hunting is a risky job. Some people prefer to camp on rocks nearby or even at the foot of the tree and then leave for the cheri at daybreak, but I like to walk back immediately."

Krishnan continued, "I like walking through the forest at night. I use a torch to pick my way, sing songs to myself or chat with my companion.

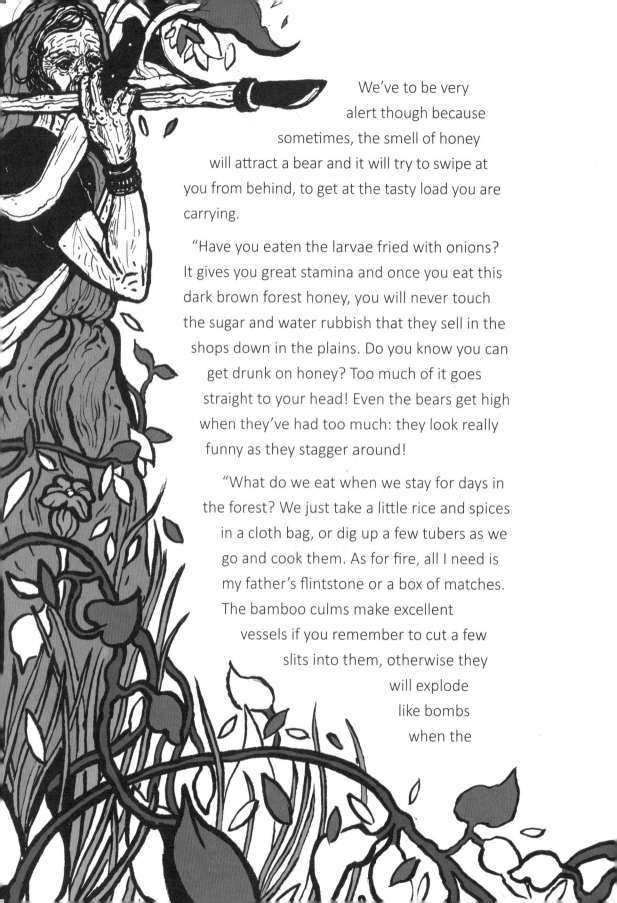

We've to be very alert though because sometimes, the smell of honey will attract a bear and it will try to swipe at you from behind, to get at the tasty load you are carrying.

"Have you eaten the larvae fried with onions? It gives you great stamina and once you eat this dark brown forest honey, you will never touch the sugar and water rubbish that they sell in the shops down in the plains. Do you know you can get drunk on honey? Too much of it goes straight to your head! Even the bears get high when they've had too much: they look really funny as they stagger around!

"What do we eat when we stay for days in the forest? We just take a little rice and spices in a cloth bag, or dig up a few tubers as we go and cook them. As for fire, all I need is my father's flintstone or a box of matches. The bamboo culms make excellent vessels if you remember to cut a few slits into them, otherwise they will explode like bombs when the food gets heated and you will have to gather your lunch from all over the forest floor in the old-fashioned way! I sometimes like to make tea in a bamboo stem because it has a different flavour – it tastes green and salty. In fact, in my grandfather's time, this was the only salt we used: we'd cut down the large stalks and scrape away the faint gray powder on each of the lids that separate the stalk into compartments. Bamboos are actually like big flavourful tiffin carriers! Don't you agree, Madiyappan?" Madiyappan nodded.

Shanti spoke up. "There were no straws in those days, so if someone wanted to drink water from the stream without all the bugs and twigs getting into their mouth, they'd use the hollow stem of a reed to suck the water up. Since the reed is narrow, only the water will enter it and all the rubbish will get left behind."

I told her, "The first time we trekked to Pandaravarai, Madiyappan told me that there's mineral water in the forest! He said the streams flow past medicinal plants, rocks, fallen fruits and heaps of elephant and gaur dung. When their essence mingles with the water, it becomes 'mineral water', which we can drink for free any time we want! No need to buy it from a shop!" They burst out laughing.

"He likes to tease you, but you must be careful about water because not all streams are fit for drinking, especially those close to pathways or roads," said Padma as she cleaned the vessels she had cooked lunch in. (Padma spends a lot of her time cleaning this and that. Vigorously.)

"We take water from streams further uphill or in the areas that we keep clean, where no one goes to bathe or wash things. We know some streams and pools that have these tiny leech-like creatures in them that can enter your body and eat you up from the inside. But the worst kind of water is found in the streams that flow through the tea and coffee estates: they don't have twigs, leaves or little tadpoles like these forest streams so they look cleaner and shine like a mirror in the sun. But they are full of pesticides."

Then Madiyappan gave me a sly smile and said, "Since you are an outsider, perhaps you can answer this question: why do tourists waste clean white paper on wiping themselves after going to the toilet instead of using all those large teak and *vada maram* leaves that are lying around for free?" Padma scolded him because she said he often talked about poop. So we changed the subject and I asked them how they found food in the forest.

Krishnan said his wife always accompanied him to collect tubers. "She will carry a long pole with a pointed blade, like a crowbar, to dig out the *chandana kizhangu* that she is so fond of. Sometimes a chattering bunch of women will go all by themselves to dig out tubers: you can tell what they have been up to even from a distance because they will wrap the pallu of their saris differently, so

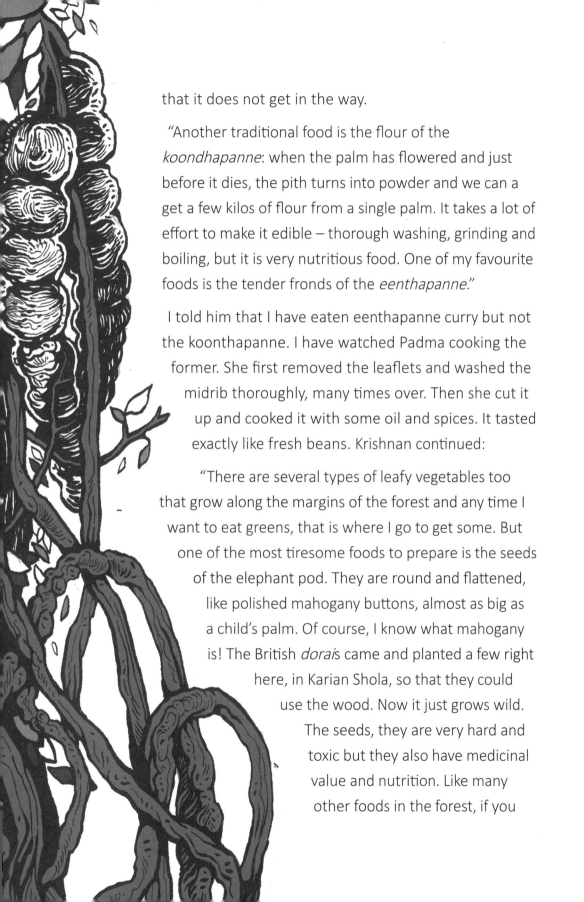

that it does not get in the way.

"Another traditional food is the flour of the *koondhapanne*: when the palm has flowered and just before it dies, the pith turns into powder and we can a get a few kilos of flour from a single palm. It takes a lot of effort to make it edible – thorough washing, grinding and boiling, but it is very nutritious food. One of my favourite foods is the tender fronds of the *eenthapanne*."

I told him that I have eaten eenthapanne curry but not the koonthapanne. I have watched Padma cooking the former. She first removed the leaflets and washed the midrib thoroughly, many times over. Then she cut it up and cooked it with some oil and spices. It tasted exactly like fresh beans. Krishnan continued:

"There are several types of leafy vegetables too that grow along the margins of the forest and any time I want to eat greens, that is where I go to get some. But one of the most tiresome foods to prepare is the seeds of the elephant pod. They are round and flattened, like polished mahogany buttons, almost as big as a child's palm. Of course, I know what mahogany is! The British *dorai*s came and planted a few right here, in Karian Shola, so that they could use the wood. Now it just grows wild. The seeds, they are very hard and toxic but they also have medicinal value and nutrition. Like many other foods in the forest, if you

know how to remove the poison, it gets transformed into something edible; it's all a matter of knowledge and skill. The white flour inside them has to be soaked for hours in water and washed repeatedly for a day or two; the old water has to be poured off each time and fresh water added. After all that cleaning, it can be made into a *kanji*. We rarely eat this now since it is just so troublesome to cook.

"After a day's work of honey-hunting, digging tubers or clearing the fire-lines for the Forest Department, we will camp in a clearing that has sheet rocks. This is the best place because we can light a big fire without the fear of setting the forest ablaze, spot an animal

before it gets too close, and there will be fewer ticks and leeches on the rocks. Otherwise, despite my tough Kadar skin, even I cannot get any sleep!"

"Of course, even we have changed since our grandfathers' times," said Madiyappan, shaking his head and stretching out his legs. "For instance, many people now go to the town to buy slippers, use soap and powder, and many of my young nephews and nieces long to live in a city with cinema theatres, cool drinks and bikes. Now, young people want to go out and see the world outside, and find people such as me old-fashioned because we still spend most of our time inside the forest.

"But the strange thing is, the more time I spend inside here, the more the world comes in search of me! I have worked with researchers, photographers, movie makers and tourists from all over the world, even when we don't have a common language. Indians from research institutes to the east, west, north and south of here; others from America, Australia, Germany, Japan – they all want to walk inside Karian Shola with me! And truly, everyone sees the forest with different eyes – some people notice only small creatures like ants and snails; others come in search of large things like elephants and tigers; still others want to see medicinal plants; some talk of 'focus' and 'contrast' and what makes a good photograph; others are terrified of leeches and ticks and find them wherever they go.

"I think this is why our ancestors said it was important to enter the forest with a clean heart, so that you find only good things on the way." Then he gave a big sigh and went off to take a nap under the jackfruit trees.

THE RETURN

Madiyappan always closes his eyes for a few seconds every time he enters the forest, so I wondered aloud if he prayed each time. Did he pray to Kadavul or to the animals? He talked as we took the trail to the Pandaravarai peak.

"Old Kadars like me chant a few lines, both when entering and leaving the forest. When we leave, we thank the muthiyar for watching over us, the forest for whatever produce we may have gathered that day and the bear, elephant, tiger, scorpion, snake and so on for keeping away from our path. Ah yes, this is a big difference between us and the outsiders: we pray that nothing should come our way, whereas they pray that everything should come and stand right in the middle of their trail! They don't realise the dangers."

He pointed to a big vada maram we passed every day.

"See, the perun thaen on that tree has been removed. We had strict rules in the olden days, about who could take what, from which area and in which season from the forest – this meant that there was always something left behind for the birds and animals, to keep the forest going. For instance, my wife is from Erumaparai so when I married her, I moved from Valparai to here and am permitted to collect honey from her family's area, which is most of Karian Shola. And we're allowed to take honey only in the dry season when there are many flowers and the bees can replenish their store, for, if we take away their honey just before the rains, they will die of hunger. And we are supposed to leave some honey behind to appease the bears, however small the hive; our old stories say that men and bears were once brothers but later had a misunderstanding and became enemies. I'll tell you that story another day.

"Many practices change with time, but I try to teach all the children who walk with me about how to exchange gifts with the forest: our survival depends on it. Of course, nowadays we eat rice and onions like the plainspeople. But at any time when we don't have money, the forest will still provide us with food for free. And medicines too, when we are ill and cannot afford to go to the hospital.

"Don't you feed the banana leaf to your cow after you eat? Or share a biscuit with your friends? And in return they look after you in different ways. It's the same here too: I share the fruit with the monkeys,

honey with the bees and bears, tubers with the wild boars and barking deer, mushrooms with the tortoises and junglefowl… it's a long list."

Later, we reached Pandaravarai and admired the view of Karian Shola below. Madiyappan said I could now climb like a tahr. At last! While he sharpened his machete on a rock, he told me very seriously,

"We return to the forest again and again and again: as much to fill our stomachs as our hearts. The first time a man climbs to get honey at night remains etched in his memory; the adventures we share with our companions keep us and our grandchildren entertained through many monsoons; the dullest day is enlivened by spotting a bird or an animal; and our spirits rise when we walk trails that take us past trees that know our ancestors.

"Remember even when we die, we come back as the glossy muthiyar to watch over our descendants as they walk the old trails."

I believe him.

AUTHORS' NOTE

The Kadar people are a forest-dwelling tribe of the Anamalai Hills in south India. They used to be nomadic hunter-gatherers but around 40 years ago, they were forced to live in small permanent settlements at the edges of these forests. However, they still continued to live off forest products and were well-known for their junglecraft. For the past 200 years, the Kadars have helped other people journey across or work in these hills, by acting as guides and labourers for traders, road builders and tea planters. As a result, many of them are familiar with different languages like Malayalam, Tamil and English — although they also have their own language, called 'aal alaapu', which literally means 'people speech'.

Even today, long treks in the forest and across the hills are an integral part of the everyday life of many Kadars, especially the elders. As they say, the very word 'Kadar' means 'people of the forest', so how could they possibly keep away? We had an opportunity to walk these forests with them — as young researchers trying to understand the different ways in which forest dwellers relate to their environment, and we were spellbound by their powers of observation and story-telling. Walking for hours with them gave us an insight into their culture and knowledge; many of the routes and places that we traversed had an historical event or anecdote, a myth or song associated with them. They all revealed something about the Kadars' relationship with plants, animals, spirits and outsiders like us.

We also found that their way of knowing the forest involved the entire body: they spoke not only of what they saw, but also what they felt, touched and smelled. Wanting to convey their dynamic and lived sense of the forest, we decided to write a book that would capture the way Kadars walked the forest. For they taught us that walking was a means of knowing and not just a mode of travel. Walking involved not only movement, but attentive observation and a sense of timing; it also required us to be acutely aware of colour, light, sound and silence in the forest. We think the Kadars are amongst the best teachers of what it means to live with nature.

Trees, plants, birds and animals described in this book are not uncommon in other parts of the world. So wherever possible, we have used the common name, such as in the case of teak and bamboo. In other instances, we have retained the Kadar or local name. Given below are some of the latter, along with their English equivalents.

Chandana kizhangu A tuber

Cheri Settlement

Dorais Masters

Eenthapanne Cycas

Gaur Indian Bison

Kadai Shop

Kadavul The Almighty

Kanji Gruel

Koondhapanne Caryota, also known as fish-tailed palm

Kungilium or Sambarani Frankincense

Langur A species of monkey that mainly feeds on leaves

Macaque Another species of monkey

Malai Malasar An indigenous community

Maram Generic Tamil word for 'tree'

Muthiyar Malabar Whistling Thrush

Naaval A purple-coloured berry

Ongal The Great Hornbill

Vada maram Terminalia tree

This book is for three friends, now whistling thrushes - Yamini, Deepa and Ravi Sankaran.

WALKING IS A WAY OF KNOWING In a Kadar Forest
Copyright © 2017 Tara Books Private Limited
For the text: © Madhuri Ramesh and Manish Chandi
For the Illustrations: © Matthew Frame
Design: Laura Nogueira

For this edition:
Tara Publishing Ltd., UK | www.tarabooks.com/uk
Tara Books Pvt. Ltd., India | www.tarabooks.com

Production: C. Arumugam
Printed in India by Canara Traders and Printers Pvt. Ltd.

ISBN: 978-93-83145-60-7